ANOREXIA NERVOSA:
THE WISH TO CHANGE

Self-help and Discovery
The Thirty Steps

by

A H Crisp
Neil Joughin
Christine Halek
Carol Bowyer

Illustrations by Nicky Browne

2nd Edition

Psychology Press
An imprint of Erlbaum (UK) Taylor & Francis

Coventry University

Copyright © 1996 by Psychology Press,
an imprint of Erlbaum (UK) Taylor & Francis Ltd

1st Edition © 1989
Department of Mental Health Sciences, St. George's Hospital Medical School.

Psychology Press
27 Church Road
Hove
East Sussex, BN3 2FA
UK

P000987
26/6/97

British Library Cataloguing in Publication Data

a catalogue record for this book is available from the British Library

ISBN 0-86377-408-3

Typeset by HH Design
Printed in Great Britain by Redwood Books, Trowbridge, Wiltshire

ACKNOWLEDGEMENTS

We should like to express our thanks to our patients, who are also our friends and who have taught us so much about this illness and how sometimes to recover from it.

We should also like to thank Nicky Browne for her skillful illustrations, some of which were based on feelings expressed pictorially by patients; and Heather Humphrey for preparing the manuscripts of both editions.

Let me be

CONTENTS

FOREWORD

There are very few specialist services for those affected with the so-called "eating disorders". Of course, it isn't only specialists who can help and it certainly is the case that specialists cannot always help. You may know only too well how difficult it is to change, with or without outside help. Moreover, those few specialist resources that exist in the UK are being increasingly restricted by managerial decisions to providing local or sub-regional services. Even so, they remain overwhelmed with referrals of would-be patients, and often can't accept them all.

This is despite the reluctance of many of those afflicted even to seek the possibility of such help or to agree to it being sought for them! So who can help? Can self-help work?

Self-help is a complicated concept. To the authors it does not necessarily mean seeking to help oneself in isolation from professional helpers or from the family. That attitude may be unconstructive and indeed characterises part of the problem underlying the disorder. Rather, the authors see self-help as meaning that the person with the problem is committed to change to a better kind of self-regulation and to shrugging off the disorder if at all possible. That preliminary step may itself open the door to such change. Then you can hopefully begin to search for possible support in the task. Mutual support can derive from contact with fellow sufferers, especially if they are also motivated to change. You could also hope that so-called experts and people themselves not afflicted (perhaps including your own family) might be available to take your hand, open doors and point the way. Of course, when it comes to anorexia nervosa, your family may need such help alongside you but this doesn't mean that you may not also be able to help each other if you decide to try.

This book confines itself to consideration of anorexia nervosa within the above framework. It complements the first author's views contained in more detail in his book, *Anorexia Nervosa: Let Me Be*, referred to in the text.

The aim of this book is to try to help you help yourself.

CHAPTER 1

WHAT IS ANOREXIA NERVOSA?
Our view and our messages

We are our parents and their bond;
please let us be fulfilled.

Hello

We want you to think carefully before you decide to give up
anorexia. The chances are that a lot of people have told you that
you will feel better if you gain weight. This may be true in the
long term, but you know only too well that it isn't in the short
term.

It may be that you don't feel you have anorexia. Some books or films offer a particular picture of the problem. For instance some people will say that they haven't got the disorder because they don't binge and vomit, as they saw happening in the film *Catherine*. These aren't necessary symptoms. More often the problem is in accepting the implications of the label of anorexia nervosa. You may fear that you will then be regarded as no more than an "anorectic" or else "just an awkward person who refuses to eat". You may feel you would be more exposed to people offering you advice or threats about the need to eat. You, and your family, would have to face the fact that there is a serious problem, which at best results in a limited life, at worst can result in death. It is easy to see why "anorectic" is a hard label to accept.

*This book has to deal with anorexia in general. It will therefore be easy to be critical of those aspects which are "not about me", and therefore ignore all the advice. This is your choice, but we think you should seriously consider the possibility that someone else **is** able to understand you — even if this hasn't been your recent experience.*

Why do people have anorexia nervosa?

Because they are overweight? This explanation is far too simple. You felt fat and overweight — but why? The majority of people have their first episodes of anorexia in their teens, and women who never develop anorexia often feel uncomfortable especially during their teens with their newly acquired body shape, wish they were thinner and diet intermittently. Very few people find adolescence and its tasks of forging an adult personality easy. It is a time of challenges. It starts, several years before the first menstruation in females, at the onset of puberty with those very changes in body shape due to body fat about which many young women, and some young men, become sensitive. These concerns can get powerfully attached in your mind to the other new experiences which come with puberty, and which, in one way or another, have become frightening for you. The end of adolescence is more difficult to identify. Adolescent problems can be reactivated later in life, for instance at the time of marriage, childbirth or death of a parent, and such events can then cause an episode of anorexia nervosa later in life. The assumption that an eighteenth or twenty first birthday marks our readiness for adulthood does not always reflect reality.

Anorexia nervosa is an unwitting reversal and thereafter an avoidance of development. It can be understood as a way of banishing insecurity and conflict, often including conflict or potential conflict between you and your family. Weight loss and loss of plumpness returns your body and its feelings to its state before puberty. Symbolically enough, if you are female, your periods stop early on or your development may arrest even before your periods have started and many of the problems of adulthood come to be completely avoided. Thus weight loss works even more effectively than a tranquillising drug or alcohol. The emotions that have been most hard to tolerate are dampened down and eliminated and a kind of security achieved. Within your state of starvation, distress is channelled exclusively into panic about losing control of your low body weight — a price you have obviously needed to pay.

Many people ask whether something to do with sex is at the bottom of the problem. The answer is yes and no. Sex is an inescapable aspect of growth into an adult. It is the product of puberty and relates to the sensitivity that many females and males develop at this stage about their bodies — with females being more concerned about their "fatness". Many people also ask whether anorexia nervosa is caused by previous sexual abuse. Such abuse has sometimes occurred in the backgrounds of those with anorexia nervosa. When this is the case it is invariably a most important influence on the condition. It can leave the affected person very fearful of their development or even deadened. But intense fear of sexuality can have many other origins. For instance sexuality may threaten a family which is too tightly bound up in itself or too distanced from the various values of the outside world which beckons the adolescent, or where parents' love is too conditional on compliance, or the family too committed to furthering your social or educational development above everything else. Then again, children may see one of their parents apparently damaged by the sexual conduct of the other parent, may even fear being like the latter parent themselves and thus cause further harm. Sex may become "bad" and relief from its impulse profound, and an especially close bond may become forged with the "damaged" parent. Such complete reversion to "childhood" as anorexia nervosa reflects may also re-cement some parental marriages which need the presence of the child in the family for their survival. As puberty develops and adolescence arises, sex can rarely be denied and becomes a major factor of either a real or imagined kind in relationships with people of your own age. If you are to feel secure in the outside world you will need to have worked out a personal solution rather than an imposed one to this dilemma. We prefer to view sex as a powerful and inescapable force but equally aim to put it in its place when trying to understand its influence. Sex in our view is best seen in terms of other human needs for love, security, respect, self-esteem, self-control, immortality, and the usual human search for intimacy that links these things. This applies not only to you but to those around you including your parents. If sex has got out of hand — becoming too stifled or too unmanageable — then an underlying question concerns what other needs are not being met.

People also sometimes ask whether anorexia nervosa is inherited. Many disorders are a product of both inheritance and development and this is true for anorexia nervosa. We touch on this in the section addressed to parents.

Coming to terms with the idea of having anorexia nervosa

As mentioned above, there is a variety of reasons for not accepting the idea that you are suffering from anorexia nervosa. It perhaps becomes a more acceptable idea if you understand the problem in a broader context than eating behaviour, and if you are clear that it is a major problem that warrants help rather than scorn or dismissal from others. Anorexia nervosa is often called an eating disorder as if this was its primary basis, and of course eating is severely disordered in it, and this may be causing great problems in the family. For instance, if your family is together then you may notice that your mother now appears to feel helpless and your father perhaps angry and helpless. However, it is our belief that the (hidden) psychological problem revolves importantly around the meaning of body shape and hence weight, and this is what you need to understand. This understanding will need to link your shape and weight with problems in your development, usually involving you and your family, which we believe underwrite the condition. They may or may not have been acknowledged at the time. Present family relationships and strains are different and will not greatly reflect the problem that existed before your anorexia nervosa developed.

You are likely to have anorexia nervosa if you have a (secret) terror of being more than about 7 stone*; less if the onset was very early in your life or you are especially short, or perhaps rather more if you are male and taller. For you, your weight is indeed the be all and end all of "being". As a result of your terror, you keep your weight down, and this results in a state of chronic bodily starvation hedged around by defences against weight gain to the exclusion of everything else.

---

* A *stone* is a unit of weight familiar to people in the UK. There are 14 lbs in 1 stone and 2.2 lbs in 1 kg. *Detailed conversions between these three measures are laid out on pp. 82-83.*

You may have got used to defiantly claiming that your condition is fulfilling, but you may in fact experience it more as a vitally necessary safe, or not so safe, retreat. This is the trap of anorexia nervosa. You are caught within a distressing way of life, but if you share your fears with other people you find, or fear, that they will not understand. You therefore say that you are "fine". You will be used to creating such smokescreens: convincing other people that you are puzzled as to why you don't gain weight, claiming that you can at last crack it by yourself, gaining a little weight at the cost of great anxiety in order to reassure others, denying to others your all-absorbing preoccupations. You need to shed such defences. They simply distance you even more from those around you. Accepting and acknowledging the idea of anorexia nervosa is necessary if you are going to tackle the problem.

The costs of anorexia nervosa

Others will not always share your apparent ease with your
situation and will try to interfere. For you yourself, as the
condition progresses, the costs become more evident. Anorexia is
a full-time job. Your preoccupation with food prevents other
activities. Friends sense that something is wrong and back away.
You fail to tackle difficult emotions that would have been
prompted by your adult body including its sexuality: for instance
in learning to cope in relationships with people of your own age
and in renegotiating your relationship with your parents. Those
people who remain in contact may do so in response to you as an
invalid, not for love of the adult you. Life leaves you behind.
Sometimes this realisation happens many years after the onset of
the problem, leaving an awful feeling that it is too late to catch up.

Males with anorexia nervosa

If you are a male with anorexia nervosa and have been reading this you may by now feel baffled and worried. How do many of the features which seem to be specifically female relate to your own problem? Is there something especially wrong with you since the condition is so rare amongst males?

The answer is that a great deal of what has been written applies to you. Loss of periods in the female is part of the early response to reduced energy intake (energy-rich food) affecting reproductive and sexual behaviour and feelings in general which is equally mirrored in you. The question is the same — what is behind this process? The answers, we suggest, are also the same and reflected in the general content and the **30 steps** presented in this book.

Males are less often concerned about their "fatness" than females but this can arise if you have been definitely fat and teased or else, sometimes, if you have been experiencing some doubt and panic about, say, your masculinity. Such gender doubt during adolescence is not uncommon and also arises amongst females, but may be less conspicuous.

As with females, we are able to tell you that it is very definitely possible to recover from anorexia nervosa and, in our view, you can best take the same steps to try to achieve this — all 30 of them!

Older patients with anorexia nervosa

Older patients with anorexia often comment that they do not feel able to relate to what is written in most books on the subject. So much of what is written is about adolescents and adolescence. We take the point. For those older people with anorexia which began in their teens the problem may not be so great, but it is still a problem. For those people with an onset of the disorder later in life the problem is quite pronounced.

If you are now older, but your anorexia began in your teens, then the origins of the disorder are presumably much the same as for other sufferers where it began in adolescence. However, elements of the problems faced by sufferers change over the years. The factors that perpetuate the illness may not be the same as those that caused it. If you have had anorexia for over a decade it will usually be the case that your life is, to a large extent, dictated by anorexia. It will mean that life centres around food, social contacts will be constrained by this and isolation may be a major problem. Too often the disorder wears down family strengths and sufferers can become isolated from their families, perhaps with a degree of mutual anger. Commonly sufferers will agree that they have the problem, but this recognition is not by itself enough to enable them to give up the disorder. You recognise that anorexia is a barren, controlled way of life, but you know little else and giving it up is terrifying. You can no longer get better and simply re-engage in school, teenage relationships, and a career. You are viewed by the world as being your chronological age, but only part of you has this maturity. The rest of you has missed out on a lot of the developmental experiences of others. If this applies to you then you are far from alone. Your reading of this book should be in the context of recognising that attempts at change should be slow, perhaps with more of an emphasis upon social change before changes in eating and weight. If getting over anorexia is too daunting then improving the quality of your life within anorexia is often very possible.

If you develop anorexia at say 25 years old or even 50 years old, how does our understanding of what causes the disorder apply to you? First, you need to review with yourself whether there is any possiblity of your having had anorexia earlier in your life. The weight biography suggested later (*see page 43*) may help with this. Second, we would return to the point that being 25 years old is not necessarily a marker of having achieved an average level of maturity for this age in all areas. Third, it may be more common in older sufferers that the anorexia is 'discovered' by accident. A period of physical illness, distress or depression may lead to significant weight loss. With this weight loss come the secondary emotional changes experienced by anyone undergoing weight loss and you may be 'hooked'. Because you are older it is then harder for others to say enough is enough. The independence of being older is a mixed blessing, making it easier to avoid interference from others but also harder to get and accept help. As with younger sufferers it does seem clear that the faster you get help the better.

A message to parents

If you are involved as parents you will probably feel helpless and very anxious. You will wonder whether you are to "blame" and whether there may still be some manoeuvre that will help your child to gain weight.

Blame is not, in our view, the right concept; nor is it a creative one. We do believe you are very importantly involved. You and your children find yourselves with inherited characteristics. These can contribute to anorexia nervosa. They may have to do with your shapes, your relationships with food, a tendency to deal with strains by avoiding them, a particular mode of thinking, feelings of anxiety and low self-esteem. Such characteristics can probably sometimes be modified or kept at bay. More important may be the ways of dealing with problems that you have developed and the nature of your relationship as a couple. Some marriages are held together by children. Other parents are insulated from the outside world, requiring this also of their children. Such conditional acceptance can place impossible strain on sensitive young adults who need to forge a link between parental values and those of the outside world. Remember, our children can help us keep in touch with an ever rapidly changing world! Have you shared your own fears and backgrounds, including your own teenage years, with them or indeed with each other? Looking again at your teens, how did you really cope and could you have done it better and less defensively? Be honest and then you may have the strength to help your anorectic child. It is easy to have misjudged your child's needs prior to the onset of the disorder. Other patterns and strains can arise within anorectic families and are touched on earlier in this book and also, in greater detail, in *Anorexia Nervosa: Let Me Be* (➜ *see Reading list p. 92*).

The book is intended for you as well as the family member with anorexia nervosa. You can have a vital role helping the anorectic to recover. Without your involvement the anorectic is more likely to feel, paradoxically it may seem, that she is betraying you if she gains weight. At the same time you may sense her anger at the situation she finds herself in. The book is intended to help sufferers understand their own anorexia and hence achieve change. This is much more possible if those around the sufferer are also able to understand the anorectic predicament and their part within this. They can thus offer support and perhaps also change. Involvement with your child does NOT mean dictating that she or he eat the kind of diet discussed, but may mean offering to provide the kind of diet discussed, and helping the anorectic to reconstruct what was happening in their lives when eating problems began. For this to be done effectively the anorectic will need your permission at the very least. Even if you have anorexia yourself, or some other major problem, e.g. a drink problem, then perhaps now is the time to acknowledge it.

These ideas can be hard to understand. When you are living with the chaos, distress or despair that anorexia nervosa can provoke and feeling that you don't know what to do, it is difficult to concentrate on these concepts. All you can think about is the next meal, and survive day to day. To think back to the past may seem irrelevant, indulgent or perhaps distressing. However it is necessary. If you do not understand how important families can be, and how they influence people, we strongly recommend a book *Families and How to Survive Them* (➔ *see Reading list, p. 96*). Remember, your anorectic child is being advised in this book to look at her or his childhood background. Perhaps you should have another look at your own childhood and adolescence. It may be painful but it may help you to recognise and identify with the present underlying problems.

A message to spouses/partners

A lot may depend on whether you married your partner before or after the development of her or his condition. You may need to reflect that the anorexia is an important requirement of the marriage. If you now want to help your partner throw it off then you will certainly need to get involved with the tasks that we have outlined here and almost certainly you will need to change yourself rather more substantially than might naturally occur. The same things apply if you are an established partner though not married.

CHAPTER 2

HOW TO CHANGE:
THE 30 STEPS

What happens if you try to give up anorexia?

Attempts to give up anorexia through gaining weight result first of all in intensified panic about your weight. If you gain more weight you may experience once again those earlier frightening and unpleasant feelings of which you had rid yourself and which have been touched on already. Yet those around you look more cheerful, as they see reassuring evidence that you are gaining weight and hope or conclude that the problem is resolved. You yourself, however, feel emotionally much worse, and often angry at others' failure to realise what you are going through. Too easily this becomes a good and necessary reason for once again retreating into weight loss. You will find lists in this book of the possible effects of gaining weight up to adult levels and also, by implication, of losing weight down to anorectic levels (*see pp. 40-41*). Later on we shall be inviting you to consider those lists in terms of yourself.

How to find out what underlies your anorexia

(STEPS 1 - 9)

Whether your aim at the present time is to escape from the grip of anorexia or to be a better adapted anorectic, you are unlikely to be able to achieve these things if you only address your eating problem and fail to recognise and come to terms, at least to some extent, with the underlying issues affecting your fear of gaining weight to a normal adult level. The following is a series of steps that we hope might help you in this latter task. Remember that, emotionally, you are certainly no older than the year that this condition developed and that you may always have been young for your age (although others may have seen you as particularly mature, perhaps because you were "good" within the more structured environment of home or school, or perhaps because you have acquired high academic or professional qualifications). *Begin now to use your diary (➔   p. 49) to record your journey up these first nine steps.*

STEP 1

Stop and think.
Could it be that your illness is helping you and others to avoid the strains of life? Remember that those strains will no longer be present — the anorexia nervosa has solved them (but brought others). ➜ Go to the *Effects of Weight Gain* exercise (*pp. 40-41*) and try to complete it in relation to your own situation.

STEP 2

Ask yourself — should I stop in my tracks now and try to unscramble things before any more time is lost? You've given up any faith that you had in other people understanding you. You can accept this or you can try again. How can you make it different next time?

STEP 3

Try and reflect who you might be if you were not now an anorectic. Reflect on what was happening around the time that you became self-conscious about your shape and began to do something about it.

Perhaps your anorexia nervosa has allowed you to preserve (or recreate) an earlier pattern of relationships and behaviour which had come to be threatened, although this may now be swamped in many ways by the new conflict over you not eating. You see, the anorexia doesn't work very well, does it? Think of it in terms of yourself and your position in the family even if you are chronologically in your twenties or thirties, or even older now.

STEP 4

Start getting to know yourself better. In the first instance tackle the Exploratory Exercises in the Work Section of this book (*pp. 39-49*).

STEP 5

Start communicating better with your parents so far as this is possible. Everyone has important aspects of their parents within them. In learning about them you will learn about yourself, including the different parts of yourself that may not be communicating well with each other! Remember your parents are in the same position as you. They may also need to communicate better within themselves and with each other. They are children of their parents. If possible ask your parents about their own adolescence. Do the Exploratory Exercises with them and talk about relevant feelings. You will not begin to find yourself until you have found them.

To learn to communicate requires opportunity and practice.

STEP 6

Therefore, use your friends, e.g. by going out with them. Try to think about this in a new way. Instead of panicking or regretting it, ask why you might be avoiding doing it.

Like many other avoidance mechanisms, anorexia nervosa can exist in the background of anorectics and their families. Other strategies include avoiding communication, avoiding social contact, dependence on alcohol and withdrawing into depression. Anorexia nervosa itself can run in families.

STEP 7

Recognise and acknowledge that your anorexia stifles unpleasant feelings i.e. protects you from such feelings through the effects of your low weight. Remember you are an expert in anorexia nervosa. What you need to do is to develop new skills.

STEP 8

You will need to begin to tolerate feeling bad and frightened. This is true for many of us but especially for you.

STEP 9

Be truthful. Do not deceive yourself even if you still have to deceive others occasionally. Beware of excuses — the reasons you will think of for not acting now will probably be quite varied. Who are you trying to fool?

STOP AND THINK

➜   We suggest you take some time now to think about what
you have learnt from these steps. You will need eventually to
make a decision about where to go from here. Do not rush into
attempts to recover unless you have considered the implications
and you have the necessary resources around you. Timing is very
important. When you feel you are ready to make a decision you
have several options. Firstly, if you are still losing weight, you
will need to stop doing so. Then you will need to decide whether
to try and hold that position temporarily, or to aim for recovery,
or to remain an anorectic in the long term. Remember that you
are making a decision for the time being — it may be that you
need longer to think about things, or do not have the necessary
resources available to you. You can always make a new decision
at another time, but it is probably true that the longer you live
within anorexia the harder it is to recover. First of all you may
need to learn how to stop losing more weight.

How to stop losing weight

(STEPS 10 - 15)

STEP 10

Consider your weight. Below 7 stones or thereabouts depending on height, anorectics feel safer but there is no great psychological need to go down very much lower if only you could be confident of steadying your weight at just below this level. Of course this is an unnatural task for your body. The great thrust in it is to grow and to develop, and to develop other impulses than simply the one to eat. It is these other potential impulses (such as the sexual impulse and the body's push to explore and assert itself) that are compounding your fear about consuming more "fuel" and gaining more weight, and lead to your fear of losing control of yourself. They underwrite your sense of incompetence and low self-esteem and feeling that you do not own your body. They may have been reduced to the impulse to eat but will intensify that because it is basically safer. However, if you surrender to it you still get very distressed because you recognise your continuing poor self-control and this is now declared in terms of your "fatness", with its sexual meanings. If you are going to recover from your condition you will need to accept your sexuality and come to feel confident with it, but that can only happen gradually. You will also need to cope with its consequences. This may include the need to learn to separate yourself more from your parents, to work out a new relationship with them and to develop your personal identity. Your anorexia will have been triggered by such challenges in the first instance.

STEP 11

Having got this far perhaps you can now begin to allow yourself to think about your eating in terms of changing it to stablilise your low weight in the first instance.

STEP 12

Some people who have anorexia nervosa simply restrict their diet but others binge as well as cutting down on food. You may do this yourself. (By "bingeing" we mean consuming large amounts of food, not eating a little more than you had planned, which some anorectics feel is bingeing.) Your bingeing is reinforced by your low weight and inadequate and irregular food intake. For instance, your body reacts to starvation with increased preoccupation with food and hunger, and if you cannot resist this, then a binge may follow. You may feel as though your control has "snapped", and you then over-compensate by eating as much as possible, usually of the foods which you have been avoiding (carbohydrates including sweet foods). You will know how distressing and frightening this experience is and that it is usually followed by vomiting to prevent weight gain. We believe that it is almost impossible to stop bingeing unless you eat regularly throughout the day rather than, say, refrain from eating during the main part of it. Your diet must therefore include some carbohydrate at every meal every day.

STEP 13

So, whether you occasionally binge, or binge and vomit, or mainly restrict your diet, you are more likely to achieve stability of your present weight in the first instance if you eat several times each day and, as has already been said and as we now repeat, you must consume a reasonable number of calories on these occasions. You may well be a great expert in the identification of calories in food. To maintain your present weight you should consume 1000-1600 calories per day (*see p. 65*), depending on your height and maturity (*see Weight Table, pp. 80-81*), and of course not vomit, use laxatives, or exercise endlessly.

STEP 14

If you have been habitually vomiting or using laxatives, you need to wean yourself off this behaviour. People find that different approaches help in different circumstances. Vomiting and using laxatives seriously upset the chemistry in your body and in that sense you will feel somewhat better when you stop. Using laxatives is also a desperate manoeuvre since it mainly gets rid of fluid and renders you unable to drink even water without your body clinging on to it and increasing your weight. Some people can simply stop these behaviours and others tail them off, and now is the time for you to do one or other of these things (➜ *see Changing your behaviour, p. 72*).

STEP 15

You will also need to tackle the problems of any excessive exercise that you have been taking. A certain amount of exercise is natural for human beings but you will know, if you are honest with yourself, whether yours is excessive, and if so you should now reduce this to normal levels as best you can, although we know your starving condition itself will probably be making you restless.

In the Work Section (*see pp. 37-49*) we suggest some guidelines which may help you change such behaviours as bingeing, vomiting, laxative abuse and excessive exercise, provided you are simultaneously working through the first nine steps.

If you are planning to stay an anorectic and simply improve your condition within it as far as possible then all that has so far been said can be of help but you should skip the next section and move on to the section starting on page 35.

How to try to recover
(i.e. gain weight to an adult level and cope with its consequences.)

(STEPS 16 - 21)

If you would like to recover from the disorder then you are going to need, sooner or later, **to begin to grow in every sense.** You may need permission for this, so seek it for example from your family and from yourself, and growth should happen slowly. You may also need help from others including professionals and so consider seeking that also. If your parents or partner can also change then this will help; much of what we are saying applies equally to them.

STEP 16

Remember once again that, emotionally, you are certainly no older than the year that this condition developed and that you may always have been emotionally young for your age.

STEP 17

Give yourself time.

STEP 18

Start using your logbook now (➔ *see pp. 51-54*). Study it and use it from now on.

STEP 19

You will need to learn about your physical self. This includes discovering that you own and are responsible for your complete and adult body, and its energy. When you eventually gain weight above that 7 stone level it also means coming to terms with your inevitable physical sexual redevelopment, and indeed eventually coming to enjoy its potential. Incidentally, we think it is very important when you reach a normal weight, that you avoid pregnancy for at least the next year or two whilst you continue to discover and develop yourself.

STEP 20

You will have to come to terms with your parents, not only in how you relate to them as people, but also in how you relate to them inside you. This involves renegotiating your relationship with them so that you can be separate from them, but also respected and loved for yourself.

STEP 21

You need to develop a general sense of your own competence. This can come from engaging in the tasks outlined in the steps, rather than depending totally on your being a successful anorectic. If you cannot achieve all the ideal goals outlined here, then doing your best is just as important.

➜   Now go back and reconsider STEPS 1 - 9 as the possible means of achieving this along with the following steps, and remember that none of the above tasks can be fully completed unless you gain weight — because this makes the emotions real rather than theoretical.

How to gain weight

(STEPS 22 - 26)

STEP 22

Set yourself a "target weight". Your target weight should be the weight of the average person in our population of your height and sex and, we suggest, of the age that you fell ill (➔ *see pp. 80-81*). We recommend this since it is at this age, emotionally speaking, that you need to pick up life again.

STEP 23

Once again, you are more likely to find gaining weight easier if you eat several times each day and consume a reasonable number of calories on each occasion. You will need to build up to an amount which will lead to weight gain in the context of normal but not excessive exercise. For the moment you should walk no more than two to three miles per day at the most and not engage in other contrived exercise. Your calorie needs are determined to an important extent by your present weight and height and you will need to slowly increase your present calorie intake. ➔ *We recommend you do this in a controlled, precise way as we have outlined on pages 63-66*. You will need to persevere with the tasks of controlling any bingeing, vomiting and laxative abuse.

STEP 24

An almost universal fear is that if you relax your restrictions on diet you will gain weight rapidly and then not stop. You therefore need to weigh yourself weekly — more often may give you misleading information, and weighing yourself too often is probably a symptom of your anorexia. Plot your measured weight (don't cheat) on a chart (➔ *see Keeping a Weight Chart, p. 56*). We would recommend a weight gain of about 1 lb (0.5 kg) per week. Less than this can be hard to monitor. More is likely to outstrip the changes that we think you need to make in parallel with gaining weight — you may then panic and rebound into losing weight.

If you have been vomiting, using laxatives or restricting how much fluid you drink then you will be dehydrated. Therefore, if you give up these behaviours you may well initially gain weight more quickly than 1 lb a week. This will mean you are "rehydrating" (taking water back into your body to bring it back to normal). This is not the same as gaining weight through eating, but can be equally terrifying. The rate of weight gain will not continue once you have "rehydrated" — the process will take a couple of weeks to stabilise (if you give up vomiting etc. completely).

STEP 25

Do not let people/parents tempt you to eat too much. It will be a long while before you can take control for granted.

STEP 26

Most people with anorexia fear that once they start gaining weight they will not be able to stop. Having reached your "target weight" it is very important that you stop gaining. Gain much more and you are certain to panic and probably feel the need to resort to a low weight again. In the Dietary Plans section (*pp. 63-71*) we offer advice about how to level-off your weight. However, being at a normal weight is only the start.

How to live at a normal weight

(STEPS 27 - 30)

STEP 27

Recognise that you cannot immediately stop having many anorectic attitudes once you get to a normal weight. On the contrary, they may be intense and only wither slowly, but we are now asking you to live with them and not lose weight. Thus a lot of other things have to change along with your weight such as those listed in the important STEPS 19-21. Keep going back over these together with your family or by yourself if you have to. Such issues are fundamental to your condition and to the possibilities for change. Progress can arise as you gradually expose your body and yourself to the realities of your problems and discover how to cope by completing the 30 STEPS. It is best if you try to change these things slowly, and recognise that the time scale must be months or years. There are no short cuts to recovering from anorexia nervosa.

STEP 28

Living at a normal weight is the hardest stage of all. You have begun to give up one identity, and probably not yet found another. You are exposed to feelings that have proved unbearable in the past, and others may be thinking that you are "cured". It is your job to help them understand how you feel, to explain how appearing physically better is not the same as feeling better.

STEP 29

Remember that humanity is made up of a rich diversity of people. No one is perfect and many of us are far from perfect. If we have all been importantly influenced by our environment then blame is not a useful concept at this stage for you or, for instance, your parents. You undoubtedly need at least one friend or other such person whom you can trust and with whom and through whom you can continue to grow. You cannot expect such a person, if indeed they are going to be strong enough to help you, to meet your every felt need at this stage. Indeed, do not rush into commitments. As we have said before, give yourself a year or two after getting your weight back. Remember you have some catching up to do first in discovering who you are.

STEP 30

Allow others to help you. As we have said, living at a normal weight is the hardest stage of all. It is now that you will need extra support to help you cope with those things that your anorexia has enabled you to avoid in the past. While this support may be available to you within your family or circle of friends, or a self-help group, it is probably worth considering allowing a professional therapist to help you at this stage. Remember, you do not have to be underweight or eating abnormally to ask for help. Help may be available from many sources (➔ *see Practical Information section, p. 57)*. If you do not hit it off with the first person you see, don't assume no-one can help, try again. It's worth it. You are worth it.

If you can't get back to a normal weight

This can happen for a number of reasons, but most often because you are unable to obtain, or accept, the support that is necessary to weather the storms of living at a normal weight. There may be an alternative. The alternative is to try to live with long-term controlled anorexia; maintaining a weight that isn't life threatening. ➔ *You may find it useful at this stage to go back to STEPS 10-15.* Consume a structured diet that minimises the risks of your eating developing into a pattern of chaos — binges, vomiting and fasting (➔ *using Eating plan A, p. 69, until you have gained weight to about 6½ - 7 stones and thereafter Eating plan B*). Find structured social outlets, such as part-time employment, to maintain contact with the outside world. Try to use this book in ways which you think are relevant to you and do some of the exercises. It may be possible for you to make limited changes that will improve things for you without your having to give up your anorexia.

This alternative has a price. Personal relationships with other people will never be normal, achievements in work are likely to be limited, and you will be faced with chronic preoccupations with food that will dominate your life. Meanwhile, try to keep in touch with others even if you can only manage those relationships which are socially structured rather than personal and intimate. Life may well get easier for you as you approach middle age and, indeed, later recovery remains a possibility, although the longer you leave it the more difficult it is fully to escape its grip.

Each of the steps contains at least one particular thing for you to do; some contain several that are very important! Now that you have read this through for the first time go on and read the rest of the book. Then if you decide to try to recover, go through the steps and identify and underline each point. As you take the steps use the margins on each page to note things down (successes and temporary failures) as well as making sure that you use the work section to your best advantage.

GOOD LUCK to you all.

Remember there is one great sportsman who, accused of being lucky, is said to have replied:

"The harder I practice,
the luckier I get".

CHAPTER 3

WORK SECTION

This section is made up of exercises designed to help you think about your anorexia in new ways, for example how it affects and is affected by your relationships with other people, particularly your family.

The exercises are divided into two groups: **Exploratory** Exercises and **On-going** Exercises. The On-going exercises need to be completed over a period of time, and can give you an indication of how you are changing. The Exploratory Exercises can in fact be completed at any time, and perhaps more than once each, but we would recommend that you do tackle them early on.

Don't try to do the exercises all at once. You need to be able to think about what you have learnt from them and to talk about this with others. You may want to repeat an exercise, either to tackle it in a different way or to do it at a different time.

You can do the Exploratory Exercises with other people. Encourage your family to get involved, perhaps by doing some of the exercises for themselves and talking about them with you. Families where there is someone with anorexia often have problems with change in relationships, or some of the relationships between family members may be skewed. You can help the other people in your family by talking about these things, as well as helping yourself (➔ *Read* "Families and How to Survive Them" *see p. 96*).

You can also do some of the exercises with friends. They are a good way of learning about other people, and about how they feel. People with anorexia often find personal relationships difficult and cut themselves off from others. These exercises are, in their different ways, about communicating with yourself and with other people.

We hope you find the exercises useful and interesting. You may want to make up some exercises of your own, or use the structured approach of the On-going Exercises in other areas of your life. We would certainly recommend that you continue to explore yourself and your life in whatever ways you feel able to.

Some of the exercises may upset you in some way. Be prepared for this. Try and find someone you can talk to about doing them, maybe a friend or your doctor perhaps. If you find a particular exercise too difficult then leave it for the time being and come back to it at another time.

CHAPTER 3a

EXPLORATORY EXERCISES

Effects of weight gain in anorexia nervosa

We have listed below some effects of gaining weight. We would like you to look at these effects and work out the "cost" and "benefit" of each — to you and perhaps others (separately). Not much is a simple cost or benefit, most items can be seen as both costs and benefits (the reason for you having anorexia is that this balance sheet meets your needs). Thus for instance "looking better" to others has advantages and disadvantages, but becomes an additional cost if everyone stops worrying about you when you know they should continue to do so.

SOME EFFECTS	BENEFIT	COST
Example: You will look healthier	People will worry about me less	People will worry about me less
You may be more hungry		
You may be less hungry		
Your sleep may improve		
You may be less preoccupied with food		
There is less chance that you will binge		
You will look healthier		
You may feel more anxious		
You may become more angry		
You will become more sexually alert and potent		
Other people will worry about you less		
You will lose your anorectic identity		

SOME EFFECTS	BENEFIT	COST
You will become more aware of what anorexia has cost you		
You will be better able to understand your anorexia		
You will relate to other people better		
You will feel fat		
You will be on the road to recovery		
You will feel healthier		
You will be less constipated		
You will often feel full		
If you are female: Your breasts will develop		
Your thighs will develop		
Your periods will return		

Draw a life map

A life map is a way of representing the course of your life, including events and experiences that have been important or significant to you. One way of doing this is to see it as a road, with signposts marking the events and experiences. Or you may like to try imagining it as a journey over mountains, stormy seas, lakes, fields etc. You could then describe the different areas that you crossed at different times in your life. Try to include what are called "developmental milestones", that is things to do with growing up, like changing schools or starting your periods — together with things that you remember as being important like losing a friend, the birth of a brother or sister, or your parents having rows. The purpose of this exercise is that it can help you to see where you had got to before you developed anorexia. You might like to draw a second map, imagining where you might be now if you didn't have anorexia.

Make a weight biography

For this exercise you will probably need to join together several pieces of graph paper to make a larger sheet. Starting at the left hand side along the bottom of the page mark out the sheet in months and years up to your present age. On the upright axis mark out stones and pounds or kilograms starting from your birthweight up to your highest weight ever. Now mark on the graph any information you have about your weight at different periods of your life. You may need to ask other members of your family for some of this information. When you have plotted all the weights you know then join them together to make a graph of your weight since birth. Then go back to add information about important feelings and events that you included on your Life Map. This exercise may help you see that events in your life may have come to be linked very closely with your weight difficulties.

Draw a family tree

Include anyone you regard as being part of your family. This will help you see the basic structure of your family and whether, for example, there are any patterns between the generations. Write in the names and ages of each person and describe them briefly. *See example on page 45.*

Example of a family tree

Eric (79)
only child - worries a
lot - needs looking
after - eats too much
of Eileen's cooking

Eileen (65)
very motherly - plump -
spends all her time
looking after Eric - very
good cook.

divorced 1979

Brian (?)
drinking problem - not
seen him for years -
Mum gets letters from
him sometimes - they
make her cry

Sarah (60)
will do anything
for anyone -
interferes a lot -
kind though -
lonely, I think

married 1960

Ellen (42)
divorced - 3 kids -
always de-
pressed - Dad
worries about her

Ian (40)
lives in Australia -
2 kids - not seen
him for years.
Eric's favourite -
a good laugh

Bryan (38)
worries a lot and
works too hard -
on heart tablets -
hard to talk to him
- expects a lot

Jane (35)
emotional - loses
her temper a lot -
plump - always on a
diet - always sorting
other people out

Julie (32)
single - thin -
graphic designer -
career woman -
beautiful

me (17)
?

David (16)
Mum's favourite - gets away
with blue murder - loads of
girlfriends - causes trouble

Ian (13)
Dad's favourite - brainy -
good at everything - gets
on my nerves

Who are you like?
Who do you want to be like?
Are there any patterns in the family?
What happens to the men?
What happens to the women?

45

Plot your family relationships

Draw a spot on a piece of paper. Imagine that this spot represents you. Then place the other people in your family around you according to how close you feel towards them now. So you should now have a central spot surrounded by several others. Repeat this exercise, remembering how things were the year before you became anorectic. The aim of this exercise is to help you see who you feel closest to and how great the distances are between you and other people in your family. It will also help you to see whether your relationships to the other members of your family have changed with your anorexia. If you find this exercise helpful you could also try to remember how things were when you were ten years old or at another time in your life that was in any way important. Look to see if there is any connection between the pattern with anorexia and other patterns.

Draw your family sitting in a circle

Imagine who would sit next to whom (you can show them by letters or boxes — you don't need to be an artist). Now draw lines between different people according to the way people communicate with each other. You might like to do this according to who is closest to whom or by the methods people use to communicate, e.g. who shouts at whom, or who gives hugs etc. Use different colours for different ways of communicating. An example is given below. Again you can repeat this as for the previous exercise, noting any differences between varying times in your life. This exercise is intended to help you look at your family relationships in another way and consider the different ways in which people communicate or fail to communicate.

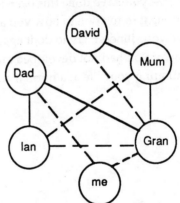

Who sits next to/opposite whom?
Who talks a lot to whom? → ○———○
Who talks a little to whom? → ○- - - ○
Who doesn't talk to whom? → ○   ○
How do you feel about the communication in the family?
Who would you like to sit by/opposite?
Who would you like to talk to you?
How would you like the communication to be different?

Imagine how other members of your family would describe you

Write down what each person would say about you. Does everyone say the same or are there differences? Check with the members of your family and find out what they think of your imaginary descriptions. You may also like to try this exercise by representing yourself visually by drawing a picture or making a collage of how other people see you. You can do this as you did the writing exercise. The purpose of this exercise is to find out whether your assessment of yourself is the same as the assessments others have of you. Often people have quite false ideas of other people's opinions of them.

Now that you have done this exercise, pause and reflect. Have you done it in relation to how you are now or how you were before your illness? Try to do it again imagining how it would all be now if you had not developed anorexia nervosa but had gone on pursuing your life at a normal adult weight.

CHAPTER 3b

ON-GOING EXERCISES

Keeping a diary

We strongly recommend that you keep a diary using, for instance, a small notebook. In this book we would recommend that you record the following information on a daily basis.

Information about your emotions that day — particularly those that arise in the context of the outlined 'Steps'. We would suggest that you avoid an emphasis on food or weight, because although these thoughts and feelings are important they are the thoughts and feelings that you are usually preoccupied with. The object of this exercise is to help you recognise new emotions and understand them in a new light. For instance you may be able to recognise emotions that on a certain day made it hard to eat.

This diary may also help you to register progress that you make, by preventing you from forgetting insights that you develop and in looking back to see how you have changed.

The diary should certainly be a private thing, but at times it may be appropriate to use this written medium to show your thoughts to another selected person. Their perspective on your thoughts is bound to be at least slightly different from your own and hence useful.

If you can begin to gain weight then other changes can arise as we have already indicated, and you may like to record these in your diary in conjunction with the on-going weight chart (➜ *see p. 56*). Try and make links between the two.

Keeping a logbook

A logbook is a tool for self-assessment which we have found useful in treating people with anorexia in hospital. It differs from a diary in that it offers a structure for thinking about key issues to do with your problems.

To keep a logbook you will need a second notebook. The logbook itself has two sections:

➢ The first offers you a series of headings and we invite you to write down your current thoughts and feelings about each heading. We suggest you do this once a week at a set time, for example Sunday afternoon.

➢ The second section is a grid which can help you to assess which areas of your life are causing you difficulty. It then asks you to identify which resources you might use to help you tackle particular difficulties. We suggest you do this monthly and, as with the rest, at a set time. You will need to copy the headings and the grid into your notebook.

We have suggested that you do these things regularly, because our experience is that people's views, feelings and preoccupations change not only with time, but also with changes in weight. You will thus be able to look back over the time you have kept your logbook and see how things have changed, as well as which things have remained constant.

SECTION ONE

The meaning of my shape to me
The trigger(s) of my illness and their meaning(s)
My family relationships; then and now
My sense of self; social and sexual
The origins of my anxiety
My use of avoidance to deal with conflict
My family's use of avoidance to deal with conflict
My other moods
Why I approach others in the way that I do
My present or future career; why I have chosen it
My relationships with authority
My impulses and the way I manage them

SECTION TWO

On page 54 you will find a list of headings in table form.
Enter your present weight at the top of the table. Consider each heading as it applies to you now and rate how much of a problem it is to you at present, using this scale:

0 = Not a problem at present
1 = More of a problem than ever
2 = No real change
3 = Some change in the desired direction
4 = Much change in the desired direction

Enter your rating in the first column.

Now choose two, or at the most three, of the problems which are causing you most difficulty at the moment. Highlight these on the chart. From the list of resources pick those which you could use to help you tackle the problem, eg. if eating with others is the problem, perhaps you could talk about it with a friend and maybe practise with them, and/or use the dietary guidelines to make a meal which you could eat with others. Tick the resource(s) you have chosen in the space provided. You now have an outline plan which you can act on.

Every month repeat this exercise (you will need to make out some more tables yourself). Write what happened in respect of the two or three problems you tried to tackle. Then rate the list again, putting in your weight as before. You can then see whether problems are resolving or intensifying. You may well decide to keep working on the same problems as before. Do not get discouraged if some problems get worse or return — this may actually be a positive sign. For example, cooking may not be a problem when you weigh 6 stones, but much more so when you are 8 stones. This is to be expected. You will probably also find that working on some problems is helpful to others indirectly.

A list of possible resources is given below. Add some of your own to this list if you have additional ones.

Resources:

G.P./Psychiatrist/Other professional help
Parents
Brothers and sisters
Friends
Partner
Self-help book
Structured exercises
Dietary guidelines
EDA/Other voluntary organisations
Reading
Painting/writing/creative activity
Social life/going out
Work
Counselling/therapy
Diary

Example of grid to use in Section 2 of the Logbook

RESOURCES

HEADINGS	Rating as a problem 0 - 4	GP/Psychiatrist /Other professional	EDA/Other Voluntary organisations	Parents	Brothers /Sisters	Friends	Partner
Asserting myself							
Being alone							
Being spontaneous							
Cooking							
Communicating							
Decision making							
Dietary education + menu planning							
Eating with others							
Expression of feelings							
Feeling in charge of myself							
Having fun							
Indulging myself							
Loving others							
My meanness							
My self-esteem							
Normal exercise							
Owning my sexuality							
Serving normal portions							
Shopping for clothes/ cosmetics, etc.							
Shopping + spending money on food							
Socialising							
Thinking of others							
Touching others							
Trusting others							

DATE: WEIGHT:

Self-help Book	Structured Exercises	Dietary Guidelines	Reading	Painting/ Writing Creative Activity	Social life/ Going out	Work	Counselling

Keeping a weight chart

We suggested that you weigh yourself once a week. It is easy to
ignore the information this provides, and we would strongly
recommend that you record your weight on a piece of graph
paper — either in pounds, or stones and pounds, or kilograms
against weeks. This chart will underline to you whether you are
gaining weight, losing weight or keeping it the same. Remember
what we said in Step 24 about a sensible rate of weight gain.

We also recommend that you draw a line across the chart
showing your target weight, if you have decided to try and gain
weight to this level, or the weight you are trying to aim at for the
time being. If you are trying to stabilise your weight at any level
(including target weight), allow a 2 lb (1 kg) band above your
chosen weight to allow for normal weight fluctuation. Aim to
keep your weight within this band.

Let us tell you that there are no mysteries to such a chart. Weight
gain or loss always occurs for an easily understandable reason —
which you will know if you are honest with yourself.

This chart will help you to notice particular difficulties in gaining
weight to a fully normal level, i.e. above the 7 stone or less
threshold referred to earlier. If you stop gaining weight before
your "target weight" then you have taken control again (by
eating less or vomiting/purging or whatever) — and you should
ask "why?" What was so difficult about continuing to gain
weight? We are not pushing you to continue gaining weight but
it is important to understand why you have chosen a particular
weight.

CHAPTER 4

PRACTICAL INFORMATION SECTION

- ◆ Energy balance
- ◆ Changing your behaviour
- ◆ Weight tables
- ◆ Professional help
- ◆ Useful addresses
- ◆ Reading list

Energy balance

Changing or stabilising your weight is not simply about what
you eat. It is a consequence of a balance between the food you eat
(and don't vomit) and how much energy you use — your
"energy balance". This is complicated by what proportion of
your body is water — your "fluid balance". To make it more
complex, vomiting and using laxatives alter the balance of salts
(electrolytes) in your body — your "electrolyte balance". Whilst
not strictly about energy, these matters are closely related to
energy, and are therefore included in this section.

FLUID BALANCE

Don't skip this section. Fluid balance is very important to
understand. It is easy to ignore because it is not about calories,
but it can drastically alter your weight. The balance is altered if
you become dehydrated for any reason. Common reasons in
anorexia include vomiting, using laxatives, restricting your fluid
intake (markedly) or using caffeine or diuretics. Excessive fluid
intake is discussed below, but it is very rare for your body to end
up overhydrated (having too much water). This is because your
kidneys cause you to produce more urine. If you are having too
little fluid your kidneys produce as little urine as possible, but
can only adjust to a certain point.

Weight loss through dehydration is confusing. Your weight goes
down, but if you drink a glass of water it may go up a by a lb. For
this reason, as well as immediate physical well-being, it is
important to avoid restricting fluid intake as a means of weight
control.

Bingeing and Vomiting

This is also dealt with in the "energy balance" and "electrolyte balance" sections. For this section it is important to recognise that in vomiting you are losing fluid. This is usually not a problem, but can be so if you do not take, and keep down, adequate water at other times. A further effect of bingeing can be a temporary increase in the amount of water in your body in response to having eaten a lot of carbohydrate. The effect is temporary, but can lead to panic about your weight going up.

Laxatives

It is important for you to know that laxatives do not rid your body of calories you have eaten by rushing food through your system in any way. They predominantly affect the large bowel which has the task of reabsorbing the large amount of water passing through it, back into the body. Laxatives irritate the large bowel and stop it from reabsorbing this water and hence users of laxatives continually pass large amounts of watery diarrhoea. Your weight will be affected by this loss of water — which must not be confused with loss of calories. Continual loss of water and essential substances like potassium (*see "Electrolyte Balance" p. 60*) lost with it leads to serious physical problems.

Diuretics and Caffeine

Diuretics are drugs that have the effect of making you pass more urine. Not everyone recognises that caffeine (contained in coffee, tea and many drinks such as Coke) is also a relatively powerful diuretic. The loss of water achieved has the same effect as laxatives, you lose weight because you lose water, but only have to drink water to regain this weight. Your weight can therefore change very quickly. Once again, this problem can make you physically ill and has an effect on your electrolytes (*see "Electrolyte Balance" p. 60*).

ELECTROLYTE BALANCE

In your body are a variety of salts, called electrolytes, one of the most important of which is potassium. Vomiting, laxatives and diuretics can all make you lose potassium. The effect of this can be very dangerous. Taking potassium replacements can be similarly dangerous. It is not always possible to gauge your need for potassium correctly, and too much potassium can be as dangerous as too little. This is another good reason to give up these particularly desperate ways of controlling your weight.

BALANCING YOUR DIET

As we state above, there is a balance between the food (and its energy content) you eat (and don't vomit) and how much energy you use. This should be a simple matter, but when you suffer from anorexia it can become very confused. It is therefore essential that you read this section carefully. A diet is not the same thing as a diet intended to lose weight, you can equally well have a diet that is aimed at gaining or stabilising your weight. Details of what we suggest you should eat are in the "Dietary Plans" section, but there are some general principles we discuss below.

Hunger and Satiety

Hunger is a concept known to everyone. Satiety is a less commonly used word. It refers to the recognition of when you have eaten enough. Both hunger and satiety are dramatically modified in anorexia nervosa.

Some people eat when they are hungry, continue to eat until they have had enough and their weight stays stable over the years.

Other people, particularly women, are constantly trying not to eat when they are hungry and stop eating before they have had enough. They will often say they are on a "diet". Commonly their weight will vary over the years. Against their expectations the tendency is for their weight to increase over time. This occurs because this constant restraint usually results in an eventual "giving in".

There is very little research on hunger and satiety in people with anorexia nervosa. This is probably because people are reluctant to tell the truth about this matter, or are badly confused. However, experience with patients tells us a lot.

You may be used to denying that you are hungry to yourself and others. For example, what most people interpret as hunger pains you report as unexplained pain. You have no idea when you have eaten enough. The concept has become very complicated. For these reasons you cannot try to get your food intake right by relying on your instincts. You are likely to always err on the "safe side" i.e. not eat enough to sustain your weight even when you have decided to try and gain. If you do want to steady your weight, or indeed gain weight, you need to take food seriously in a new way. You need to eat very regularly, and rather repetitively. It is for this reason that we offer rather concrete advice in the Dietary Plans that follow. Sadly, it will be a while before food can again be simply enjoyable.

Vegetarianism
Ask yourself "When did I decide to become vegetarian?". If the answer is since you became anorectic, then it is likely the reasons for it lie with an avoidance of fat and calories and restriction of choice. It perhaps has given you a legitimate reason for saying "no" to eating the same food as your family. It is worth

examining your reasons carefully and allowing yourself to slowly reintroduce meat and fish.

If the answer is before you became anorectic then we have included sufficient alternatives to meat and fish in the meal plans. Vegetarianism and weight loss do not have to go hand in hand, but it can be harder to provide the calorie intakes we suggest. For example, a plate of vegetables looks a lot, but has a small calorie content for its size and therefore does not constitute a meal.

Exercise

Increased exercise in anorexia is common, and it occurs for a number of reasons. One of these reasons is an attempt to "burn off" calories. Therefore, whether you are aiming to stabilise your weight or gain weight you may very well be tempted to increase the amount of exercise you are doing when you make changes to your diet. The dietary plans will only be of value to you if you do not increase your exercise. The more active you are the more calories you will need.

Bingeing and Vomiting

If you vomit after a meal or binge and vomit at any time you must eat your next planned meal or snack. Otherwise, by skipping the next meal you will be even more hungry and therefore more likely to binge or overeat soon after, continuing a very vicious circle.

Fluid intake

You may have become accustomed to drinking large quantities of fluid throughout the day to fill you up and avoid feeling hungry.

An adequate amount of fluid is between 1.5 - 2 litres (8 - 10 cups) drunk throughout the day. Avoid drinking just before you eat.

For males with anorexia nervosa :

All the advice in this section and the "Dietary Plans" applies to you also. However, at any weight men have more muscle tissue than women do and as a result of this need more calories. Therefore you are likely to need the higher dietary plans to gain weight.

DIETARY PLANS

We have attached three dietary plans:

      A   contains between 1000 - 1100 kcal
      B   contains between 1500 - 1600 kcal
      C   contains between 2000 - 2100 kcal.

The plans are as precise as is practicable when providing a varied diet. However, the variety of foods is deliberately limited as we know you will find it difficult to make choices about what you eat. You may find it easiest literally to rotate the choices given on a daily basis.

We suggest you eat three meals every day with small mid-meal snacks where stated. You may be worried about eating breakfast having got used to eating only at the end of the day. Each of the dietary plans ensures you can eat both at the beginning and the end of the day. Define your mealtimes to ensure you know when you are going to eat and don't make excuses about insufficient time to do so.

Each plan contains a snack meal at lunch and a cooked meal in the evening; these can be exchanged if it fits in better with your lifestyle. Each meal, whatever the calorie content, contains starch, protein and vegetables together with fruit and/or dessert. Many anorectics will eat large quantities of vegetables and/or salad. A plate piled high with vegetables leaves little room for other foods, therefore make an effort to put vegetables on your plate after you have served the portions of other foods. Alternatively, limit yourself to 3 tablespoons of cooked vegetables OR a side plate/individual bowl of salad.

You may find buying ready-prepared single portion meals easier than cooking for yourself. There is now a wide variety available most of which have the calorie content stated on the pack. For this reason we have recommended which meals to buy, by the calorie content, to fit in with each of the plans.

You may find it useful to see the dietary plans as prescriptions as, whatever stage you are at in the process of recovery, food is a necessary part of your overall well-being.

Which plan?

The dietary plans have been carefully thought out to allow you progressively to increase your calorie intake by slowly increasing the number of portions of the same foods you eat. In addition a limited number of different foods are slowly incorporated.

If your weight is well below 7 stones then your calorie requirements will be very small. We would suggest you take plan A and slowly increase your present diet to that level initially. Please note that a diet containing only 1000 kcal or less is not nutritionally complete enough with respect to the micronutrients i.e. vitamins and minerals, for long term use. There is a risk this would lead to deficiencies. There is very little known of the requirements of someone living at a lower than normal body weight for long periods of time, in some instances many years. If you do continue to eat such a low calorie diet you will need more specific dietary advice with respect to vitamin and mineral supplementation.

If you are going to try to stabilise your weight in the region of 6 - 7 stones, then depending on your age and height you will need to eat between 1000 - 1600 kcal per day, outlined as plans A and B. Therefore we suggest you start with meal plan A and slowly increase the portions as outlined until you are eating the diet that maintains your weight. Make only one increase at a time so that you are gaining weight in a controlled way. You will see from your weekly weight chart what effect the increase has on your weight. If your weight remains the same for two weighings then this is the time to increase your intake again so that you are gaining weight in a controlled, stepwise manner. Be honest with yourself and ensure you are eating everything as stated on your plan at each stage: no more and no less.

If you are going to gain weight past 7 stones then start with meal plan B and, in the same way as above, slowly increase your intake to that of plan C. Remember, make only one increase at a time to see what effect it has on your weight. Taller women and men are more likely to need a higher calorie intake than 2000-2100 kcal (plan C) to continue gaining weight.

To increase your intake above plan C add the following foods into your eating plan one at a time in the same way as previously suggested according to your weight gain. These foods will gradually increase your calorie intake to between 3000-3100 kcal. Taller women and men are more likely to need this higher calorie intake.

1.   ½ a portion of milk at bedtime.

2.   2 digestive biscuits mid-morning.

3.   Any 2 digestive biscuits to be replaced with
      1 bar of chocolate
            e.g.   4-finger Kit-Kat
                    or a Twix bar
                    or a 50g bar of chocolate

4.   1 boiled egg plus 150 ml fruit juice at breakfast.

5.   1 slice of bread plus 1 teaspoon of butter/margarine at
      lunch.

6.   Pudding and custard to replace individual dessert
      e.g. small fruit pie with 2 tablespoons of custard; or
            2 tablespoons of fruit crumble with 2 tablespoons
            of custard.

7.   ½ a portion of milk at mid-morning.

Plan your meals the day before or weekly so that you know what
you are going to eat. Use the eating plans to do this and stick
with your plan! Do not leave your decisions until mealtimes as
you are likely to find it very difficult to then make a choice.

You know you can run rings round these guidelines if you
choose to. If you want to change you will need to be honest here.
Coping with these changes in your diet and their effect on your
weight and shape will enable you more effectively to confront
and to begin to deal with all the other issues bearing on your
anorexia nervosa, even if your present intention is not to shed it
completely.

How to eat at a normal weight

Once you have reached your target weight the next step will be to learn how much food you need to maintain it. We know how worried you will be about continuing to gain weight above target weight, and going out of control. It is for this reason we have recommended you gain weight in the stepwise manner so that you know how much to eat to maintain it before making the next step up each time. As you approach target weight in this way it will not be necessary to decrease your diet to stop gaining weight but rather to stop increasing it.

It is all about getting the balance right between how much to eat and how much activity. You will need to learn to maintain your weight within your "target band" and this will mean tolerating small weight changes, i.e. your weight fluctuating up and down along a straight line without you making sudden and drastic changes to your diet. It is important that you continue not to vomit and purge and that you limit your exercise. We recommend you do not involve yourself in any regular, formal exercise or sport until you have had a considerable period of time learning to maintain your weight without it, say six months.

The main reason why anorectics exercise is to burn up calories and there will be a strong temptation for you to decrease your diet if you feel you are inactive or have a compulsive feeling of having to exercise to justify eating, particularly as you try to hold your weight steady. It is important for you to know that nearly threequarters (75%) of everybody's calorie intake is needed just to keep them alive, not running around.

It is going to take a long time before you will be able to rely on feelings of hunger and satiety to guide you. You may not even experience or recognise feelings of hunger at a normal weight for some time. There are going to be many mealtimes when you do not "feel like eating"; the reasons for this are more likely to be related to feelings of worry or anxiety, panic about eating too much or going out of control. It is because these feelings get confused and you become focused on how much or how little to eat at these meals that we strongly recommend you eat according to your eating plan in a prescribed manner for as long as it takes.

Only then does it become safer to begin to take risks and learn to eat in an unplanned way, for instance at a friend's house or in a restuarant, for an occasional meal if you have the familiar structure surrounding you.

Allow yourself very slowly to introduce other foods into your plan, especially foods you like!

EATING PLANS

	A No. of portions	B No. of portions	C No. of portions
BREAKFAST			
cereal	1	1	1
bread	1	2	2
fat	1	2	2
jam/marmalade	-	-	2 teaspoons
MID-MORNING			
fruit	-	1	1
LUNCH			
bread	1	2	2
protein	1	1	2
fat	1	2	2
salad/vegetables	✓	✓	✓
fruit	1	1	1
chocolate biscuit	-	-	1
MID-AFTERNOON			
fruit	1	-	1
digestive biscuits	-	1	2
EVENING MEAL			
starch	1 ½	1½	2
protein	1	2	2
fat	1	1	2
salad/vegetables	✓	✓	✓
fruit	1	-	-
dessert	-	1	1
BEDTIME			
digestive biscuit	-	1	2

(➔ *See overleaf for details of what constitutes a 'portion'*)

Conversion factor: 1 fluid oz = 25 ml
                       1 oz = 25 g

STARCH

1 PORTION IS:

Bread:	1 slice from a large medium-sliced loaf: wholemeal (wholewheat) or white	
Potato:	jacket (baked) or boiled (100 g)	
	mashed:	1 rounded tablespoon
Rice:	boiled:	2 rounded tablespoons (weight before cooking 25 g)
Pasta:	boiled:	2 rounded tablespoons (weight before cooking 25 g)

Breakfast Cereals:
1 PORTION IS:

Branflakes OR cornflakes:	25 g
Weetabix:	2
Muesli:	25 g

PROTEIN

1 PORTION IS:

For lunch:	Eggs:	1 (size 2)
	Cheese :	Cheddar type 25 g
	Cottage cheese:	100 g
	Baked beans:	2 tablespoons
	Tuna fish:	50 g
For evening meal:	Red meat:	50 g cooked weight
	Chicken:	50 g cooked weight
	White fish:	100 g cooked weight
	Beans eg. kidney, haricot	
		100g after soaking or tinned
	Lentils:	25 g (dried)

FAT
1 PORTION IS:

Butter/margarine:	1 teaspoon
Vegetable oils:	1 teaspoon
Low fat spreads:	2 teaspoons
Mayonnaise:	1 teaspoon
Oily salad dressing:	1 teaspoon

MILK
1 PORTION IS:

Full cream (whole):	300 ml
Semi-skimmed (2%):	450 ml

FRUIT
1 PORTION IS:

Apple OR orange OR Pear:	1 medium
Banana:	1 small
Fruit juice:	150 ml
Soft fruit e.g. raspberries/strawberries: 150g	

DESSERT
1 PORTION IS:

1 individual pot or portion of dessert such as (fruit yoghurt,
NOT 'DIET' VARIETIES rice pudding, trifle)

A dessert such as the above should contain between
135 - 150 kcal

Vanilla ice cream: 2 scoops

CHOCOLATE BISCUIT
1 PORTION IS:

Individually wrapped chocolate biscuit

e.g. Penguin biscuit:	1
2 finger Kit-Kat:	1
Chocolate chip cookies:	3

Ready prepared meals for the evening meal:

	A	B	C
Calorie content:	250-300 kcal	350-400 kcal	450-500 kcal

Changing your behaviour
-Bingeing, vomiting, laxative abuse, over-exercising.

These suggestions may help you if you want to stop, say abusing laxatives, but find that you can't just give it up then and there.

There are two 'golden rules' about changing your behaviour this way:

♦ **Go slowly**

♦ **Try to change a little at a time**

We say this because there will be powerful reasons why you are behaving as you are and it will take time to adjust to not behaving this way.

WHAT ARE YOU DOING?

This question might seem obvious, but you need to be clear about your behaviour before you can change it. For example, if you are bingeing, how often are you doing it, how long does a binge last, what happens afterwards, what sets it off? We suggest you keep a diary for at least one week, in which you note down the behaviour under these headings (or choose others if you feel they are more suitable):

> What time did it start?
> What was I doing before/when it started?
> How did I feel before/when it started?
> What did I do then?
> How long did I do it for?
> How did I feel while doing it?

What made me stop?
What happened after I had stopped?
How did I feel afterwards?

ESTABLISHING PATTERNS

When you have done that you should have to hand a very clear
and detailed description of the behaviour which you would like
to change. Remember that it's important to fill the diary in
throughout the week and not guess or put down what you think
is happening from memory.

Look at what you have written. Are there any patterns to your
behaviour? Do you do things at the same time of the day or in
similar situations? Do you always feel the same? What stops you
doing it? Do you always do things the same way when the
behaviour occurs? Does it relate at all to your current efforts in
relation to STEPS 1 - 9? Just identifying some of these things *may
be helpful in breaking the pattern (➜ see p.75).*

If there are no established patterns, or very few, then your first
step is probably to try and regularise your behaviour. This will
make it easier to tackle change. Here are some suggestions:

> ➢ Try to keep to regular times — either periods of the day
> (e.g. morning/evening) or specific times
> (e.g. 6-9 p.m.). Aim for a regular pattern such as
> every day or every other day or once a week, even if
> that means slightly increasing the number of times
> the behaviour occurs. You are aiming for some
> measure of control — that is, you decide when the
> behaviour will occur. Try not to do it outside the
> times you have set.

> ➤ Try to do the same thing every time the behaviour
>   occurs — for instance eat the same amount of food,
>   do the same amount of exercise, take the same
>   number of laxatives. Try not to do it in a more
>   ritualistic way than you have been doing — again,
>   the aim is that you decide what you are going to do.
>   It also means you may have to plan it.

> ➤ Try to make sure the behaviour occurs in the same place
>   every time, so that you always binge in the same
>   place, take the same route for jogging, take the
>   laxatives in the same place.

While you are 'free' of the behaviour, in between times, then try
to make sure that you look after yourself, especially in those
areas which might be suffering as a result of what you are doing
— like getting some rest if you are over-exercising, drinking
enough fluids if you are dehydrating yourself, eating your 'usual'
diet in between binges or after vomiting. You may find this hard
to do, but we recommend that you try.

CHANGING THE PATTERN

First make a list of things which you could see as rewards for yourself. Try not to choose any which are related to food, eating or exercise. They may be social contact with others, hobbies or activities, shopping, going to the cinema etc., as well as small things, like using a certain perfume, having a bath, doing your hair, or writing letters. You will need small rewards as well as bigger ones. You will be using these to reward yourself for the changes you are able to make. If you have trouble doing this, then ask someone to help you. As with most of the work in this book, it's easier to tackle these things if you have help and support from others, especially your family, and it's especially relevant when trying to change your behaviour.

You should by now have a pattern of behaviour which you want to change. You are going to try to change it in stages. First you need to identify which part you are going to change and how you are going to change it. You will have to decide this for yourself, using the information you've gathered so far, for example:

> You are bingeing and vomiting three times a day. You decide to try to cut it down to twice a day. You know that you can sometimes manage to get through the morning without bingeing. You decide to try not to binge before noon, but to keep to the bingeing on the other two occasions each day.

> You always vomit straight after every meal. You decide to try and wait 10 minutes after each meal before going to the toilet to vomit.

or:

> You are taking 50 laxatives a day. You decide to take 40 a day.

Write down what your behaviour is at present.
Then write down what you want it to be, as in the examples above. Try to change only one thing at a time. Use your diary and your identified pattern to help you find alternatives for the behaviour if necessary. For example, if other people being around stops you vomiting, make sure you are with others when you are trying not to vomit, at least initially. Be aware of what things help you make changes, so that you can use them in future.

Every time you succeed, allow yourself a small reward. Use a chart if you find that helpful. When you have managed to achieve the change for a whole week, allow yourself a bigger reward. You can then decide to make a further change, if that seems appropriate. Do this in the same way as before.

You may think that this method is too slow, or the changes insignificant. However, it is not just the actual change that is important, but also the process of being able to change. You may well have felt that nothing could be done, or that you could never control these aspects of your behaviour in a healthy way. So just being able to make any change could be important in itself. For this reason you may find that changes get easier after a while, or that you can make bigger changes at a time. Guard against pushing yourself too hard, though.

IF YOU CAN'T CHANGE OR YOU GET STUCK

Don't expect to be able to change something immediately, or without any hitches. You have to practise! Allow yourself three or four weeks of trying. If you still can't do it, then was it for one of the following reasons:

> Did you try to change too much at once?
  If so, try to make a smaller change.

> Did you try to change the most difficult thing?
  If so, try to make an easier change. You don't have to take the hardest option.

> Did you choose the right time to make changes?
  If not consider whether you are ready for change at the moment, or whether you are too preoccupied with other things.

> Did you have enough help?
  Maybe you tried without help, or need help with other aspects of your life, (e.g. STEPS 1-9), so didn't have enough resources to make the change.

> Do you need a rest from changes?
  If you find you get stuck after making some changes, then consider the possibility that you may need a break from changing. Try instead to maintain the changes you have made for a while.

> Do you really want to change?
  This may seem like a tough question, but repeated failure brings up the possibility that the part of you that does not want to change at present is too powerful. You may need help to work out why that is so.

These are only guidelines to help you and they can't possibly be comprehensive. You will need to work out your own timetable for change and we hope that some of these suggestions will prove useful. Again remember that you don't have to change everything at once and that change is usually difficult. Gradual, stepwise change may prove to be the best option in the long run. Try to be patient and allow yourself plenty of time.

Weight tables

The tables below are intended to help you realise the weight at
which you should aim. As we mention elsewhere, we
recommend that you look at the weight for someone of your sex,
your height, and your age at the onset of your major "dieting".
This will be a "normal weight" based on figures for a normal
population in the UK gathered in the 1940s. Contrary to what
you may think, these weights are lighter than more recent
surveys. We recommend these weights because they are more in
keeping with what people want (as opposed to what they are),
they may be healthier, and because experience shows that they
have been successful in helping people to overcome anorexia. We
are not recommending your target weight as the weight at which
you will feel best, look best, live longest or whatever. It is a
weight at which you stand the best chance of avoiding the
emotional and physical costs of anorexia. We feel sure that you
will argue with these figures, but we warn you that your
objections are likely to spring defensively from your anorexia.

We do not give weights for people with an onset before the age of
15, or after the age of 27. Before the age of 15 the body is growing
at very variable rates for different individuals, and hence general
advice is hard to give. An onset of anorexia after 27 does occur
but is rare. If you are unsure it is probably advisable to discuss a
target weight with your local doctor, or look in *Anorexia Nervosa:
Let Me Be* for further details.

FEMALES:

Height (ins)	15	16	17	18	19	20	21	22	23	24	27
					Age	lbs					
56	84	90	94	96	97	98	98	98	98	99	100
57	88	93	97	99	100	101	101	102	102	102	103
58	92	97	101	102	103	104	104	105	105	106	106
59	96	100	104	105	106	107	108	108	108	109	109
60	100	104	107	109	110	110	111	111	111	112	112
61	104	107	110	112	113	114	114	114	114	115	116
62	108	111	113	115	116	117	117	118	118	118	119
63	112	114	117	118	119	120	120	121	121	121	122
64	115	118	120	121	122	123	124	124	124	124	125
65	119	121	123	125	126	126	127	127	127	127	128
66	123	125	126	128	129	130	130	130	130	130	131
67	127	128	129	131	132	133	133	133	134	134	134
68	131	132	133	134	135	136	136	137	137	136	137
69	135	135	136	137	138	139	140	140	140	140	140
70	139	139	139	141	142	142	143	143	143	143	144

MALES:

Height (ins)	Age										
	15	16	17	18	19	20	21	22	23	24	27
	lbs										
60	96	99	103	106	109	111	114	115	116	117	118
61	101	104	107	110	112	115	117	119	120	121	121
62	105	108	111	113	116	119	121	122	124	124	125
63	109	112	115	117	120	122	124	126	127	128	129
64	113	116	119	121	124	126	128	130	131	132	132
65	117	120	123	125	128	130	132	133	134	135	136
66	122	124	127	129	132	134	135	137	138	139	140
67	126	128	131	133	135	137	139	140	142	142	144
68	130	132	135	137	139	141	142	144	145	146	147
69	134	136	139	141	143	145	146	148	149	150	151
70	138	140	143	145	147	148	150	151	152	153	155
71	143	145	147	148	150	152	153	155	156	157	158
72	147	149	151	152	154	156	157	158	160	160	162
73	151	153	155	156	158	159	160	162	163	164	166
74	155	157	159	160	162	163	164	166	167	168	169

UNITS OF WEIGHT CONVERSION TABLES

lbs	stone	lbs	kg	lbs	stone	lbs	kg
56	4	0	25.4	86	6	2	39.0
57	4	1	25.9	87	6	3	39.5
58	4	2	26.3	88	6	4	39.9
59	4	3	26.8	89	6	5	40.4
60	4	4	27.2	90	6	6	40.8
61	4	5	27.7	91	6	7	41.3
62	4	6	28.1	92	6	8	41.7
63	4	7	28.6	93	6	9	42.2
64	4	8	29.0	94	6	10	42.6
65	4	9	29.5	95	6	11	43.1
66	4	10	29.9	96	6	12	43.6
67	4	11	30.4	97	6	13	44.0
68	4	12	30.8	98	7	0	44.5
69	4	13	31.3	99	7	1	44.9
70	5	0	31.8	100	7	2	45.4
71	5	1	32.2	101	7	3	45.8
72	5	2	32.7	102	7	4	46.3
73	5	3	33.1	103	7	5	46.7
74	5	4	33.6	104	7	6	47.2
75	5	5	34.0	105	7	7	47.6
76	5	6	34.5	106	7	8	48.1
77	5	7	34.9	107	7	9	48.5
78	5	8	35.4	108	7	10	49.0
79	5	9	35.8	109	7	11	49.4
80	5	10	36.3	110	7	12	49.9
81	5	11	36.7	111	7	13	50.4
82	5	12	37.2	112	8	0	50.8
83	5	13	37.7	113	8	1	51.3
84	6	0	38.1	114	8	2	51.7
85	6	1	38.6	115	8	3	52.2

UNITS OF WEIGHT CONVERSION TABLES

lbs	stone	lbs	kg	lbs	stone	lbs	kg
116	8	4	52.6	146	10	6	66.2
117	8	5	53.1	147	10	7	66.7
118	8	6	53.5	148	10	8	67.1
119	8	7	54.0	149	10	9	67.6
120	8	8	54.4	150	10	10	68.0
121	8	9	54.9	151	10	11	68.5
122	8	10	55.3	152	10	12	69.0
123	8	11	55.8	153	10	13	69.4
124	8	12	56.3	154	11	0	69.9
125	8	13	56.7	155	11	1	70.3
126	9	0	57.2	156	11	2	70.8
127	9	1	57.6	157	11	3	71.2
128	9	2	58.1	158	11	4	71.7
129	9	3	58.5	159	11	5	72.1
130	9	4	59.0	160	11	6	72.6
131	9	5	59.4	161	11	7	73.0
132	9	6	59.9	162	11	8	73.5
133	9	7	60.3	163	11	9	73.9
134	9	8	60.8	164	11	10	74.4
135	9	9	61.2	165	11	11	74.8
136	9	10	61.7	166	11	12	75.3
137	9	11	62.1	167	11	13	75.8
138	9	12	62.6	168	12	0	76.2
139	9	13	63.1	169	12	1	76.7
140	10	0	63.5	170	12	2	77.1
141	10	1	64.0	171	12	3	77.6
142	10	2	64.4	172	12	4	78.0
143	10	3	64.9	173	12	5	78.5
144	10	4	65.3	174	12	6	78.9
145	10	5	65.8	175	12	7	79.4

Professional help

The good news is that there are many sources of professional
help open to you in the UK. The bad news is that the type of help
available varies tremendously and it is not always easy to hit on
what is right for you. Some help is available on the NHS and
some you will be asked to pay for. This section is intended to give
you a little more guidance about what is available and what to
expect from the various areas of help. If it is difficult to know
what sort of help to choose then ask someone to go over the
options with you and discuss them. Remember that any help
which is going to be useful is not going to make you feel wholly
comfortable — sometimes it may be very challenging — but
ideally it should offer you some sort of support as well as
working towards change. Remember too, that there are no
'magic' solutions which are suddenly going to make things
better. As we have stressed elsewhere in this book, you need to
give yourself time to change and it will take time. Be prepared for
that.

NHS SERVICES

Primary Health Care Services — available through GP
Your General Practitioner is usually your first port of call for
access to NHS services. He or she can either try to help you
directly or refer you to a hospital doctor or therapist. Other
people who may be attached to your GP's practice are a dietician,
a counsellor, and a community psychiatric nurse. Ask your GP
what is available in your practice, depending on what sort of help
you need. If there is nothing suitable then ask to be referred to a
consultant who has some experience with psychiatric or
psychological problems or who is professionally interested in

eating disorders. You can also ask to be referred to a psychologist if that seems more appropriate, or to a psychotherapy department if there is one in your area. Your family may also be able to receive help from these sources. GPs who are fundholders can refer you where they think best, otherwise they may be constrained by contracts to refer you to a particular service.

NHS Hospital Services

At present, most hospitals in the country have responsibility for defined geographical areas (catchment areas) which they serve. This can limit your choice in the first instance. You may be referred to a medical consultant or to a psychiatrist and this will affect the type of treatment approach, which will also depend to some extent on the severity of your anorexia. Some hospital services will pay more attention to physical problems and your eating, whereas some will also help you with your emotional and psychological needs. On balance, you are more likely to get help for both from a psychiatric service.

Emergencies

It is not uncommon for people suffering from anorexia to be admitted to hospital as a result of a crisis, and they may then find themselves either on a medical ward for rehydration or emergency refeeding or perhaps in a psychiatric hospital on a Section of the Mental Health Act (which means they can be kept in hospital for their own good even if they don't want to be there). There is no doubt that these can be very unpleasant experiences, but those around the sufferer may well feel that there is no alternative at the time. Sufferers themselves are most likely to seek urgent medical help if bulimia is getting out of control. Under these circumstances you may not be seeking help to shed your anorexia nervosa but to sustain it! We are in no doubt that it is preferable to ask for help for your anorexia before things get out of hand like this.

Out-patient treatment

When you are referred to a hospital, and it is not an emergency, you will be seen first in outpatients, or occasionally at home. The purpose of this first meeting is to try and work out what the problems are and how best to help you. If you want help and your physical state is not putting you at risk, then you may well be offered out-patient treatment, either individually or with your family. It is our experience that most anorectics would prefer this option, and it's certainly less drastic than coming into hospital. However, such a preference may be dictated by good or bad (evasive) reasons. It certainly means you have to take a lot more responsibility for helping yourself and working on things at home. For some people it's the best option at this stage but for others it's not enough. Out-patient treatment may be provided by various people such as doctors, psychologists, social workers, nurses and dieticians. In some cases you may be allocated a community psychiatric nurse who will come and see you and your family at home.

Day-patient treatment

Some psychiatric hospitals have day-patient units where you can get intensive support without having to come into hospital. Usually they involve you going every day of the week for a time. Often they work in groups and may also include individual and family work. Occupational therapy is also used a good deal. They are a useful bridge between out-patient and in-patient care.

In-patient treatment

For some people admission to hospital will be advised or become necessary. In most cases this will happen because out-patient treatment is not working or because it would not or does not provide enough support for the sufferer. (Some people need more support than others.) Many anorectics are very afraid of this option because they see it as threatening their control over their anorexia. However you should expect that most doctors and nurses genuinely want to help people with problems and it is worth giving them a chance. You'll need to bear in mind that they are not perfect and also that anorexia is not one of the most common problems that they have to deal with, so they may not have a lot of experience in dealing with your particular anxieties and difficulties. However, there is no reason why they shouldn't learn from helping you!

Specialist eating disorder units

There are about a dozen hospitals in the country which have in-patient units specialising in the treatment of eating disorders. More hospitals are now developing specialist out-patient services. They have grown up somewhat randomly and tend to be attached to large teaching hospitals. Predictably, the South of England is best served by such units. Some of them operate strict catchment area criteria while others will see people from other areas but are limited in their resources and by the demand on their services. Most of them have quite long waiting lists for appointments, which means they can't usually help in emergencies. Treatments available are usually out-patient and in-patient, although more hospitals now offer specialised day-patient services. Approaches to anorexia do vary between the units. If you would like to be referred to such a unit, then ask your GP or the hospital doctor you are currently seeing. You can always telephone the units to ask them for information about their services.

PRIVATE TREATMENT

Private hospital services

There are a number of doctors and hospitals which will treat anorectics privately. Some of them have specialist eating disorder programmes. They are usually expensive and may not be an option unless you have private health insurance, although some health authorities now have contracts with private hospitals. You can ask your GP for details of private hospital services and doctors, or ask in your local library for a directory of such services.

Private counselling and psychotherapy

Counselling and psychotherapy are, in our view, important aids to recovery from anorexia (➜ *see STEP No. 30, p. 34*). There are many private therapists and counsellors across the country and it can be difficult to know how to choose someone suitable and reliable. Such help is not always cheap, but usually much less expensive than private medicine, and many counsellors and therapists charge sliding scale fees according to your income. Again it may be worth asking your GP or someone in your occupational health department if they can recommend someone — most trained therapists are not allowed to advertise their services directly to the public. Perhaps someone in your school or your church may also know of a good counsellor, or the local Citizen's Advice Bureau may have a list. The Eating Disorders Association hold a list of counsellors and psychotherapists who are willing to help people with anorexia. ➜ *Other such resources are listed on pages 90-91* . When you have found someone, be critical. For you especially, it is important that you work with someone who will take your weight and eating seriously, and not all counsellors and therapists feel happy about getting involved with those issues. Equally it is important that you like and feel supported by the therapist, at least in part. If you feel you really can't get on with someone, then look again. It's vital that you find someone you can learn to trust and depend on.

Family and marital/couple therapy can also be obtained privately. ➔ *See the resource list on pp. 90-91 for contacts.*

Other private treatments

There are a variety of other treatments which people try, like acupuncture, hypnotherapy, relaxation, massage, allergy treatments, homeopathy, etc. The same advice applies as for private psychotherapy. Some of these treatments, for instance those which help with relaxation, can provide useful additional support to someone who is trying to come to terms with life either at normal weight or as an anorectic. Some of them are, frankly, useless to an anorectic and may cost a fortune. Beware of any treatment which claims certain success or quick results. We and you know that things are much more complex than that. So, as you can see, getting the help you need and want may not always be straightforward. As we said before, don't give up if you can't find the right help immediately. This book itself reflects one of our own efforts to help you and others like you who wish that things could be better in these respects.

Useful addresses

EATING DISORDERS ASSOCIATION

Sackville Place
44 Magdalen Street
Norwich
Norfolk NR3 1JE
Tel: 01603-621414

The Eating Disorders Association is a nationwide organisation
which aims to offer help and advice to sufferers and their
families. They offer a telephone helpline, answer letters and have
a huge list of resources available to people suffering from eating
disorders. They also run a network of self-help groups for
sufferers and sometimes their families. They publish a regular
newsletter for members.

BRITISH ASSOCIATION FOR COUNSELLING

37a Sheep Street
Rugby
Warwickshire CV21 3BX

The BAC can give you advice on finding a reputable counsellor
or therapist in your area. They also publish an annual directory
of such services, which you should be able to get from your local
library.

RELATE (formerly the Marriage Guidance Council)

Herbert Gray College
Little Church Street
Rugby
Warwickshire CV21 3AP

Relate offers counselling to people who are having relationship
difficulties (not only those who are married). Their counsellors
are well trained and there is a branch in most areas. Look in your
local telephone directory or contact the above address for more
information.

INSTITUTE FOR FAMILY THERAPY

43 New Cavendish Street, London W1M 7RE
Tel: 0171-935-1651

This is a training organisation for therapists which also offers
family therapy and mediation services to clients. Self-referrals are
accepted and fees charged on a sliding scale.

THE WOMEN'S THERAPY CENTRE

9 Manor Gardens
London N7

The Women's Therapy Centre offers low-cost therapy for women
as well as day and weekend workshops, some of which focus on
eating problems. They work from a feminist standpoint which
might not suit everyone. You can get an idea of their approach
from reading Marilyn Lawrence's book (➜ *see Reading List,*
p. 93). Write to them for details of therapy and workshops.

Reading list

BOOKS ON ANOREXIA NERVOSA

Anorexia Nervosa: Let Me Be
by A.H.Crisp
published by Lawrence Erlbaum Associates

Our general approach is reflected in detail in this book. It attempts to link the social, cultural, personal and physical aspects of the condition both in terms of its development and its treatment. Against this background, towards the end of the book, ten patients, and sometimes their families, describe their own experiences of the condition. You may want to read these first. Then have a go at reading the book through. The author suggests that "Anorexia nervosa is a biological solution to an existential problem". What do you think?

The Golden Cage
by Hilda Bruch
published by Open Books

This book is a classic of its kind. We differ in our views only in degree from Dr. Bruch who presents anorexia nervosa as the "pursuit of thinness" as though this was a choice of identity rather than a flight to a refuge permitting no alternative. She also emphasises the primacy of food rather than body shape in her attempt to understand the factors that precede anorexia nervosa during childhood and to relate them to the illness. We suggest you read this alongside *Let Me Be*, searching out the differences and similarities of approach.

Anorexia Nervosa
by R.L.Palmer
published by Penguin Books

This is a very useful and comprehensive book which aims to help you make some sense of anorexia nervosa and also of any hospital treatment you have received or may be thinking of trying. It is written by a doctor and concentrates largely on medical approaches to anorexia, but it doesn't do this in a narrow-minded way. It is easy to read and should help you and your family be better informed about anorexia.

The Anorexic Experience
by Marilyn Lawrence
published by The Women's Press

This book is written by a therapist at the Women's Therapy Centre in London. She has had a great deal of experience in working with women suffering from anorexia and her views are based on a feminist approach to the problems young women face in life. Her approach is in no way extreme and the book offers a useful, non-medical way of looking at anorexia. It is readable, informative and encouraging and includes plenty of examples of women's differing experiences of having anorexia. The book invites you to choose whether or not to tackle your difficulties and how to find a way of doing this that suits you, in a very supportive way.

The Art of Starvation
by Sheila MacLeod
published by Virago

This book should be seen as consisting of two parts. The first part involves Sheila MacLeod's very personal description of her childhood and the experiences she sees, with hindsight, as being important influences on her subsequent anorexia. Her account of family life and her school days is particularly evocative and well written.

The second part, or aspect, of this book revolves around the author's own view of how and why people develop (choose) anorexia as a means of coping and self determination. In this she discusses theoretical issues, as well as her own attempts at recovery. This is quite technical at times, and generally harder going for the reader.

Overall, a worthwhile book, which would probably benefit from being read around, and shortly after, the time of reaching target weight.

Hunger Strike
by Susie Orbach
published by Penguin Books

This well-written book offers a sociological and cultural view of anorexia nervosa. Written from a feminist standpoint, it sees anorexia as a cry of protest against the demands placed on women in today's society.

Eating your Heart Out
by Julia Buckroyd
published by Optima Books

This book is about eating difficulties in general, not just anorexia, and it is aimed at helping you think about what underlies your eating disorder. It is easy to read and develops some of the ideas contained here. It should set you thinking!

Getting Better Bit(e) by Bit(e)
by Ulriche Schmidt and Janet Treasure
published by Lawrence Erbaum Associates

An excellent book intended to offer direct help to people with bulimia or problems with binge eating. It is highly educational and offers advice on a wide variety of areas. Some topics are obviously central, others are less obvious but are known to be vitally important in recovery.

Video: Recovery from Anorexia Nervosa.
During this hour-long video, Professor Crisp talks with individuals who are now fully recovered from anorexia nervosa and willing to share their experiences, including their feelings of hopelessness and helplessness within the illness. It is only available for personal and group educational purposes, and can be purchased on enquiry from the following address:
Mrs H. Humphrey (Assistant to Professor Crisp)
Psychiatric Research Unit
Atkinson Morley's Hospital
Copse Hill, London SW20 0NE.
Tel: 0181-725-4154

BOOKS ABOUT FAMILIES AND RELATIONSHIPS

Families and How to Survive Them
by Robin Skynner and John Cleese
published by Methuen

This is a very popular and charming book which explains simply
and clearly the process of development of the personality and
how this is affected by the family's established patterns of
communication.
It describes in an amusing and entertaining way basic
psychological concepts. We highly recommend this book which
has particular relevance to your attempts to understand your
personality, your family relationships and the ways in which you
relate to others.

Games People Play
by E. Berne
*published by Deutsch. (Also available in paperback, published by
Penguin Books)*

This book is about the different ways in which people relate to
each other. The author looks at them as "games" in which the
participants "agree" to take on different roles according to what
they hope to gain from their relationships. People tend to play
similar roles even in different relationships. This book can help
you look at the way you relate to others and how they in their
turn relate, both to you and to other people. You may be able to
find patterns of relating. The book is fairly scholarly, but is also
intended for a wider audience.

BOOKS ABOUT SEXUALITY AND RELATIONSHIPS

First Love, First Sex: a Practical Guide to Relationships
by Kaye Wellings
published by Thorsons Publishing Group

This book is recommended by the Family Planning Association,
and is a clear, comprehensive and readable guide to all aspects of
intimate and sexual relationships. Although its title suggests it is
a "beginners book", it nevertheless contains a lot of information
of use to anyone who has anxieties about or difficulties with
intimate relationships. It is full of illustrations and well worth
buying for yourself.

Girls and Sex;
Boys and Sex
by Wardell B. Pomeroy
published by Penguin Books

These books are written from years of experience counselling
young people on sexuality. They are direct and informative and
aim to explore this area in an explicit and unembarrassed way.
They are very readable and can help to allay a lot of anxieties
about sexual feelings and behaviour.

Friday's Child
by Carol Lee
published by Thorsons Publishing Group

A personal account of sex education for teenagers in schools
which is readable and particularly sensitive about the neglected
male angle.

BOOKS ABOUT BECOMING AN ADULT

Everygirls' Lifeguide
by Miriam Stoppard
published by Dorling Kindersley

This book is informal and chatty and deals with many aspects of growing up, both physically and psychologically. It is well illustrated and easy to read. Its main fault is that it tries to cover too many areas at once, and we think that some of them are treated rather superficially, but it would do as an introduction.

A Woman in Your Own Right
by Anne Dickson
published by Quartet Books

This is a clearly written, informative book looking at ways in which one can become more assertive by developing clear and direct ways of communicating. Particular areas addressed are saying "no", handling criticism, managing the expression of anger, sexuality and assertiveness, and how body language conveys feelings.
If you are male, you can read this book with advantage. It will tell you how many women feel and it may also help you to define yourself better.

The Blind Side of Eden
by Carol Lee
published by Bloomsbury

This is a book about men and women written by a woman. It is perceptive, clear and uncompromising. It can help many of us get a firm, more accurate view of ourselves through such processes as telling us how others see us. Read the last page first and then be prepared to put your feet up.

BOOKS ON SEXUAL ABUSE

As we mentioned in the text, sexual abuse has sometimes been experienced by people suffering from anorexia. Because this is a subject which is especially difficult to approach, we are including some books which might help you in thinking about it, and eventually talking about it, if relevant.

I Know Why the Caged Bird Sings
by Maya Angelou
published by Virago

If I Should Die Before I Wake
by Michelle Morris
published by Black Swan

These two books are written by people who have personally experienced sexual abuse.

A Girl like Abby
by Hadley Irwin
published by Plus Fiction

This book is a novel about sexual abuse and dealing with the experience.

Too Close Encounters and What to Do About Them
by Rosemary Stones
published by Piccadilly Press

This is a book about how to keep yourself safe and what to do if you find yourself in a dangerous or uncomfortable situation. It is easy to read and very practical in its approach.

BOOKS TO HELP WITH SOME OTHER PROBLEMS AND DIFFICULTIES ALSO ASSOCIATED WITH ANOREXIA NERVOSA

Human Aggression
by Anthony Storr
published by Penguin

This book sets out to explain why anger and aggression evolved, and their value in many situations. It describes what happens to people when they are angry, and goes on to discuss how people are affected by anger when they can't express it.
It is a rather technical book, but we wanted to include something about this area of emotional experience because it's something anorectics usually have a lot of difficulty with. It is quite easy reading, and not long, so even if you find it hard to see yourself in the descriptions, give it a try.

Depression. The Way Out of Your Prison
by Dorothy Rowe
published by Routledge & Kegan Paul

At some weights you may be spared depression, but as you gain weight or come out of anorexia nervosa you are certain to experience new feelings of hopelessness and helplessness. This can be frightening and it is likely that neither you nor your family have the skills to deal with such an episode. This book will help you recognise what is happening to you and what you can do about it. The book may also be useful to parents who are experiencing depression — as you begin to recover. If you feel that they are being helped then you can go on recovering.

Also by Dorothy Rowe:
Wanting Everything, and **Beyond Fear**
both *published by Harper Collins.*

Coping with Depression
by Ivy Blackburn
published by W & R Chambers

There are a lot of books designed as either self-help manuals or information sources. This book seems to provide a balanced view of how most professionals perceive depression. It discusses available treatments and makes suggestions about what you can do to help yourself.

Living with Fear. Understanding and Coping with Anxiety
by Isaac Marks
Published by McGraw-Hill

Anxiety and being afraid are central to our understanding of anorexia. This book is not specifically about anorexia or even eating disorders. It is about severe anxiety more generally, and offers advise about how to manage specific fears and obsessive compulsive disorder. Symptoms of the latter are common in patients with anorexia. You should be able to find a lot in this book to apply to your problem.

USEFUL FICTION

There are very many novels written about relationships and feelings with which you might be able to identify and which you might find it helpful to read. We give just an introductory selection below.

The Secret Diary of Adrian Mole Aged 13¾
by Sue Townsend
published by Methuen

The Death of the Heart
by Elizabeth Bowen
published by Virago

The Summer After the Funeral
by Jane Gardam
published by Penguin

The Rainbow
by D.H. Lawrence
published by Penguin

The Catcher in the Rye
by J.D. Salinger
published by Penguin